GENTLE MERCIES

Hal Haralson

Run So That You May Win
ivictor.com

Victor® is an imprint of Cook Communications Ministries,
Colorado Springs, Colorado 80918

Cook Communications, Paris, Ontario

Kingsway Communications, Eastbourne, England

GENTLE MERCIES

First Printing, 2001

Printed in the United States of America

2 3 4 5 6 7 8 9 10 Printing/Year 05 04

Editors: L.B. Norton; Craig Bubeck, Sr. Editor

Cover Design: Alan Furst, Inc.

Interior Design: Alan Furst, Inc.

Like Jesus' parables, Haralson's stories are subterfuge, slipping in under your guard and seizing you with such truth, grace, and extravagant love, you will never be the same again!

George Cladis, Presbyterian Minister, Darien, CN

The book can serve any public speaker with illustrations full of truth and power. Gentle Mercies will surely impact your life, as it has mine.

Howard Hovde, Director Emeritus, Laity Lodge

Hal Haralson's moving narratives are a testimony to how God speaks through our lives, satisfying our hunger to hear His voice.

Paula D'Arcy, author of Song for Sarah, *and retreat leader*

My first anxious reading of Gentle Mercies was so fast and furious that I devoured it. By the third reading, I was able to slow down and take the time to relate to names and places—I laughed and I cried.

Laura Graham, mother in the story Being There

Hal Haralson's words will provoke your thought, evoke your tears, and warm your heart. He reminds us all of what's really important in life.

Lanny Hall, President Hardin-Simmons University

Here's a mix of sorrow and joy, tragedy and triumph. Hal's wisdom, courage, and faith are a glory to behold.

Howard Butt, Jr., President H.E. Butt Foundation

God wanted Hal as he was, and that's how you'll find him here. I think God just might grab you through Hal Haralson.

David Redding, Presbyterian Minister and author of over 20 books

How is it that Hal makes me laugh and cry at the same time? Maybe it's the cowboy in each of us that loves campfire stories.

Keith Hosey, Catholic Priest and Director of John XXIII Center

I find these Christian stories written from the male perspective excellent, and I want to get a book for each of my three sons.

Dianne J. Pinkelman, OH

TO JUDY

For forty-four years my wife and companion,
through the bad part and the good.
Your love is the greatest gift I have ever received.

And to Jill, Brad, and David, our children,
who went through it all and came out as adults that make us proud.

MY DEEP GRATITUDE TO . . .

Browning Ware, my childhood hero, cousin, and pastor.

Dale Haralson, the brother who has shown me that one can be a Christian and a good trial lawyer, and for turning Judy over to me.

Linda Quinn, for over twenty years my secretary, legal assistant, and friend.

Foy Valentine, editor of *Christian Ethics Today*, for encouraging my writing and giving me a place to put it.

Paula D'Arcy, author, speaker, and newfound friend who has encouraged my writing.

Howard and Barbara Dan Butt, whose love and generosity to me and my family through Laity Lodge and the youth camps have made this journey more meaningful for all of us.

Laura Graham, whose love and friendship spans forty years, and for allowing me to tell her story.

Weston Ware, who has been a friend for life and has shared this journey with me.

Keith Miller, who has been friend, mentor, and encourager since he first asked me to speak at Laity Lodge in 1965.

David Redding, my teacher whose "write from the lump in your throat" produced my first story at Creative Week at Laity Lodge.

Bill and Betty Ann Cody, David, and Cathy. I am the blessed recipient of the love and creative insight of this family. Even after Bill's death, we all are blessed by the use of the Cody Center at Laity Lodge.

Keith Hosey, the only Catholic priest I know. My thanks for sharing the journey with me and Judy.

the people of the First Baptist Church of Loraine, Texas. They shaped my life for eighteen years, and the foundation proved to be strong.

Lanny Hall and Jesse Fletcher and all the teachers at Hardin-Simmons University who showed me what I could do (especially Emogene Emory).

Hull and Carolee Youngblood, who sheltered us when we were young and going through the most difficult time in our lives.

Buckner Fanning and the people of Trinity Baptist Church of San Antonio, who supported us during our darkest hours.

Roger and Suzie Paynter and our church family at First Baptist Church, Austin, Texas, for their love and support.

Harry Lundell, close friend and hunting companion for twenty years. Thanks for the memories.

Ken and Cathy Jones, friends whose love we've shared for many years.

To laugh often and love much; to win the respect of intelligent persons and the affection of children; to appreciate beauty; to find the best in others; to give of one's self; to leave the world a bit better, whether by a healthy child, a garden patch, or a redeemed social condition; to have played and laughed with enthusiasm and sung with exaltation; to know even one life has breathed easier because you have lived. This is to have succeeded!

—Ralph Waldo Emerson

CONTENTS

PART ONE

Stops Along the Journey

The Private
Was a Preacher

Following graduation from Hardin-Simmons University in 1957, I volunteered for the draft. Judy and I had been married six months, and she followed me to Ft. Riley, Kansas; Ft. Leonard Wood, Missouri; and "advanced individual training."

The wisdom of the U.S. Army placed me in Ft. Gordon, Georgia where I went to Military Police school. I learned how to shoot a 45-caliber pistol and direct traffic. I can still make it flow with the best of them.

Our permanent station was White Sands Proving Ground, New Mexico. We lived in nearby Las Cruces because there was no base housing.

We hadn't been there long when there came a phone call one Saturday night.

"My name is J.W. Ray. I'm a member of Westside Baptist Mission. We are sponsored by First Baptist Church. We have twelve members and we meet in an Oldfellow Hall. Could you come visit us in the morning?"

I assured him we could. This was exciting. I had been preaching for about five years, and Judy and I had hoped to be involved in a mission.

When J.W. Ray introduced me the next morning, it was obvious he meant more than "visit." He wanted me to preach!

All of us who have preached have two or three "sugar sticks" we can deliver standing on our heads. So preach I did. They called us as pastor and wife at a salary of $25.00 per month.

There was only one problem with this arrangement. My military police duties called for three-day shifts. I was only off on Sunday one-third of the time.

I went to the colonel (base commander) and explained the situation, asking to be assigned to an eight-to-five job. To say he was not sympathetic is a bit of an understatement. In fact, he emphatically declared that he would not make an exception on my account.

I did some research. Army regulations said if an enlisted man's duty assignment interfered with his worship, he must be reassigned if there is an opening. It didn't take me long to find the opening. An MP who was making security badges was about to be discharged. His was an eight-to-five job.

I typed a memo to the base commander citing the regulation and attached a letter from the association missionary that authenticated my claim to being an ordained minister. Also attached were letters to two congressmen and a United States Senator . . . but it turned out that I didn't have to mail them.

As I stood at attention, the colonel read my memo. He was furious—but the transfer was made.

Now that the church had a pastor, I knew that what we needed next was a revival! I called my mentor, Leonard Hartley, and he agreed to come and preach. Dressed in my MP gear, I took the information about the coming revival to the base newspaper. "What are you doing bringing a story about a revival?" asked the man at the paper. I told him I was the pastor of the church. He asked some questions and took notes. Then he asked if he could take my picture in the pulpit of the base chapel . . . with a 45-caliber pistol on my hip.

Two weeks later the story came out in daily papers in El Paso, Albuquerque, and Alamagordo. "White Sands GI Pastors Church." That was the boost we needed. The revival was a success, and we were off and running.

By the time Judy and I left Las Cruces on June 11, 1959, with my discharge papers in hand, Westside Baptist Mission had become Westside Baptist Church. We had baptized 75 people and built a church that would handle 200 in Sunday School. It was full. All of this had happened in eighteen months. The congregation called a full-time seminary graduate as pastor. He stayed seventeen years.

This is one military policeman who is thankful he was given more to do than direct traffic. ∎

The View from a Padded Cell

I lay on my back on the mattress and looked around. The ceiling was padded. The walls were padded. I was cold, but I had no clothes because I was dangerous to myself.

For a nearly a year I had struggled with depression. I would spend days in bed, then I would have a manic period where I seemed invincible. Our doctor finally told Judy, my wife of five years, six months pregnant with our second child, to take our four-year-old Jill and go home to be with her parents for Christmas.

December 16, 1963. Monday morning. No one in the house but me.

I turned on all the gas jets in the bedroom and went to bed. The gas exploded and set fire to the house . . . and I was committed to the San Antonio State Hospital, a "failed suicide attempt." The hospital would be my home for the next three months.

What led to my depression? For two years, I had wrestled with questions about my "calling" as a pastor without telling anyone of my dilemma. I was sure at age sixteen that God had called me to preach, and I was told that there is something special about this call. College and seminary preparation had reinforced that feeling. Could God's call to me have changed?

I had never failed at anything in my life. Yet I wanted out of the ministry and strongly sensed that this was not what God wanted for me now.

But what of Judy? She had married me because she felt God calling her to be a minister's wife. If I left the ministry, how would that affect her?

What of the long years of preparation for this vocation? My education had all been for the ministry. I had graduated with a 3.6 grade point average and been president of the student body my senior year at Hardin-Simmons University. Would all that be wasted?

What would the people of the two churches I had pastored for the last ten years say? Would I be considered a failure? How would I make a living for my family?

My mind raced around and around after these questions as I lay on my bed in my padded cell. My mental illness was diagnosed as manic-depressive (later as bipolar). After six weeks in the hospital, and thirteen shock treatments, my psychiatrist said that if I didn't find another line of work, he felt I would attempt suicide again or spend years in the state hospital.

I made the decision to leave the ministry and was released from the hospital five days before the birth of our second child, Brad. Soon after I was released, Ed Bush, an Episcopal priest who was a member of the prayer group Judy and I were in, came to my house. "Hal," he announced, "I have two things to say to you. One, be of good cheer. Two, everything is going to be all right."

I knew my illness would be a part of my life as long as I lived. Other, shorter hospitalizations would be necessary over the years when depression would reoccur, but I was taking lithium and in the care of a good doctor.

It was as if God said to me through Ed, "I have been here all along. I will never leave you or forsake you."

I didn't know that day where God would lead, but I knew that I would awaken each morning thankful for a new day . . . and thankful that my bedroom was not a padded cell. ∎

Starting Over

I woke up in the middle of the night, fear gripping my body. All I could think of was one huge question: Now what?

I was back in the same house—214 Brookview, San Antonio—where three months before I had attempted suicide.

I had cut loose from the only profession I had ever known after ten years in the ministry.

I now had not only a wife and a daughter to support, but a wife, a daughter, and a newborn son.

We were deep in debt because of my not working for the past four months.

I had to find a job . . . but doing what? I had never done anything but preach. I listed my abilities and experiences:

1. I was a good public speaker. With ten years in the ministry, I was comfortable in any public speaking setting.

2. I had experience advising students regarding college and job placement. This came from my job in public relations at Hardin-Simmons University after my stint in the army.

3. I was reasonably intelligent, I figured. I'd graduated in the top 10 percent of my college class.

4. I was a good counselor. In the two churches I had served as pastor, I had logged many hours helping people with their problems.

Now . . . to find someone who needed these skills. There had to be someone out there if I had heard God right. He had a job for me and would not abandon me.

For the next two months I spent at least eight hours a day job hunting. Newspaper ads, tips from friends—I followed every lead I received.

Each time I was interviewed I told the prospective employer about my skills. I also told him about my suicide attempt and stay at the state hospital. I could not be honest and keep this from a prospective employer. I felt then, and still do, that honesty is the only way to go when dealing with mental illness. It takes the pressure off and reduces the stigma that is so often a problem.

I usually heard, "We will get in touch with you"—polite way of saying "We wouldn't touch you with a ten-foot pole!"

Somehow I was not discouraged when I was turned down. Instead I felt that that was one more job I knew was not for me, and I was one step nearer the one that was.

I kept looking, thankful to my parents and Judy's parents for helping us meet expenses, knowing my job was out there somewhere.

Then one day while I was out, Judy took a message asking me to call the office of Lloyd Flood. Who was Lloyd Flood? The name was not familiar to either of us.

When I returned the call, I found I had reached the office of Montgomery Ward. Mr. Flood was the district manager, and he wanted to set up an interview with me.

At first I didn't think I'd bother to go. Montgomery Ward meant ladies' shoes and pots and pans. I wasn't interested in either of those things. But I had made a commitment to investigate every opportunity offered me. So I went.

Mr. Flood was a dignified man who knew his skills as an interviewer. He asked about my background, work experience, and skills. Then he asked if there was anything else I felt he should know. I told him about the suicide attempt and the state hospital. He indicated he appreciated my honesty. He gave me an application to fill out and said he would be in touch.

The standard brush-off.

Two days later I got a call from Mr. Flood's secretary asking that I meet with the company doctor and return the application.

Judy and I grew excited. We worked together on the application and allowed ourselves to wonder if there was a real possibility of a job here. We talked about how much to ask for where it said "salary requirements." We worked out a budget that would allow us to pay our expenses and concluded that we could get by on $300.00 per month (remember, this was 1963). Since I figured I'd be lucky to get half what I asked for, I asked for twice what I hoped for . . . $600 per month.

The physical examination with the company doctor went well. I thought he was a little too curious about the suicide attempt and state hospital, but other than that it was appropriate.

Then came the call for another interview with Mr. Flood.

His secretary showed me in, and he indicated one of the comfortable chairs in the office. Then he came from behind his desk and sat so there was nothing between us.

"Hal," he began, "I need to be honest with you, just as you have been honest with me. I can't pay you the $7,200 per year you requested. Do you think you could start at $6,500 if I guaranteed to raise you to $7,200 after six months?"

I have to admit I was a little dishonest with good Mr. Flood. I hesitated, as if this were a difficult decision to make, and then I replied, "Yes, we can make it on that."

"Good," he said. "Now I'd like to tell you what position I have in mind for you." This was the first time anything had been said about what my job would be.

"I have calls constantly for someone to speak at civic clubs and schools. I'm not comfortable in that setting. I think you would be.

"We have 600 employees, and there is a constant need for someone to listen to the problems in their marriages and with their children.

"Also, employees get into conflict with each other, and

someone needs to hear them out and settle disputes.

"Finally, I need someone who can interview applicants and place them where they can benefit themselves and Montgomery Ward the most.

"Hal, I want you to be director of personnel and public relations."

I thanked Mr. Flood and said I'd be at work the next day.

Then I went home to weep and celebrate with Judy.

Mr. Flood had just described a job that allowed me to use every experience I had had up to that point in my life. He had just confirmed my belief that, if I had read God right in leaving the ministry, there was a place waiting that would allow me to use my gifts and experience.

I worked for Mr. Flood for two years. During that time I received two promotions and the entire state of Colorado as my territory.

An answer to prayer? God takes care of His own?

I think so.   ■

Perfect Timing

My friend looked at me and asked, "What would you do if you could do anything you wanted to do . . . money is no object?"

I was thirty-three years old, married, with children ages one, five, and ten. "I'd go to law school," I replied.

"How much would you and Judy need a month?"

This was August, 1968. "We could probably get by on $750 per month," I said.

"How about a thousand?"

"Okay . . . let's make it a thousand."

Within two hours we had worked out a contract whereby he and his partner bought my interest in a real estate brokerage business, paying me $1,000.00 per month for thirty-six months.

The next Monday I was looking at the sign on the door of Dean T. J. Gibson at the University of Texas School of Law: "Do not knock . . . come in."

I introduced myself to the man who was always there for students. He looked as though he had slept in the clothes he wore.

I introduced myself and told him I wanted to go to law school.

"When do you want to start?" he asked.

"When does school start?"

"Two weeks. When did you file your application?"

Uh-oh. "I haven't filed an application. I only found out two days ago I was going."

"What did you make on the LSAT?" Dean Gibson asked.

"What's the LSAT?"

The dean looked at me and slowly shook his head from side to side.

"Look, Dean," I said. "I'm thirty-three years old and married with three kids. I've been out of college over ten years, but when I was there I had a 3.6 grade point average while holding down three jobs. I've got enough money to do this over the next thirty-six months. If I'm going to do it, it's got to be now."

"All right," said this wonderful man, "I'll tell you what I want. You write me a letter. Put what you have told me in that letter. I'll present it to the admissions committee on Thursday, and I'll call you on Friday."

The call came. "You're admitted. You have to pass the LSAT in November."

During my third year of law school, I was on the admissions committee. I learned then that between 1960 and 1970 there were three times as many applicants as there were openings at U.T. Law School . . . except for the fall of 1968. The Vietnam War had taken so many undergraduates that there were still openings when school began.

There are times when the presence of God is felt in events in a way that cannot be explained as coincidence.

This was one of those times. ∎

Hiring Cornelia

If you are in the top 10 percent of your graduating class in law school, you have a job. You are hired by a partner in a law firm who graduated in the top 10 percent of his class and was hired by a partner (now deceased) who was in the top 10 percent of his class.

I graduated from the University of Texas Law School in 1971 with a 71 average . . . nowhere near the top 10 percent of my class. (In my defense, there was a good reason for that. Although I'd had excellent grades in high school and college, I'd vowed that I was not going to be an absentee father and husband for three years in order to excel in law school. My rules were no study at night, no study on weekends—just an eight-to-five day, Monday through Friday. I had a wife and three children who came first.)

I graduated right on schedule, three years after I began. But no one wanted to hire an old man of thirty-seven who had graduated in the bottom third of his class. So I hung out a shingle on South Lamar in Austin in September of 1971 and began practicing law.

I listened, took notes, and kept my mouth shut, and people assumed I knew what I was doing. If I were stuck I'd say, "This is a difficult question. I'll have to do some research and get back to you." Then I went back to the books and found out what to do.

My system worked! Soon I had clients . . . lots of clients. I needed a secretary. I ran an ad in the paper: "Experienced legal secretary. Growing law firm. Salary negotiable."

Enter Cornelia George. Cornelia had worked for former Governor Dan Moody for ten years, then for a well-known appellate attorney for fifteen more. He had died about six months earlier, and Cornelia had closed his office.

She was the first to call and the first to be interviewed. She was impeccably dressed. I guessed her to be about fifty-five.

"Cornelia," I said, "You are just what I want, but I can't afford the $15,000 a year you've been making. I'm only paying $400 per month."

Cornelia studied a moment. "Promise me you won't hire anyone until I call you tomorrow," she said.

"Done," I replied.

The next day she called and asked, "When can I start to work?"

At the end of six months, I had hired two lawyers, several secretaries, and was doing work for over 100 clients.

And then it happened. Remember Carl Sandburg's poem, "Fog"? I had learned it in high school:

> The fog comes
> on little cat feet.
> It sits looking
> over the harbor and city
> on silent haunches
> and then moves on.

I remember sitting at my desk, overwhelmed by all those clients, and feeling the depression moving in on little cat feet. It had been six years since I was depressed. I had thought it gone.

Eventually I closed the office and let everyone go. But when I told Cornelia, she said, "You'll be back. I won't take another job. I'll be ready when you need me."

After six months I began again, gradually. I would take

work to Cornelia's garage apartment and pick it up the next day.

When I reopened the office with Cornelia, I had new rules: no work after five o'clock, no work at night, and no work on weekends. (I've kept a secretary past five P.M. one time in 25 years.)

Cornelia was with me seven years. One day I asked her how she came to answer my ad in the paper. She told me she couldn't work for six months after her employer died and she had to close his office. He was an alcoholic. It was very difficult.

"Then one day I decided it was time to go back to work. I prayed and asked God to help me to find a lawyer who was a Christian, someone for whom the practice of law was more than just making money. For the first time in my life, I picked up the paper and looked at the employment want ads. I saw only one—yours. After our interview, I prayed again, and I knew."

"But the salary . . . Cornelia, you had been making $15,000 per year."

"The salary wasn't important. I have lived in the same garage apartment for twenty years. My only recreation is visiting the members of my Sunday School class at First Baptist Church. When I started working for you, I was sixty-five and on social security. I didn't need the money."

Then and now, I find myself in awe. The people on the journey are all placed there. There are no accidents. ■

Mom Goes
Back to School

Judy had decided early in life that God was calling her to be a pastor's wife. This, among other things, qualified me to be her husband, and we were married in 1956.

Judy was the kind of person people were drawn to and felt safe with. She loved her role as pastor's wife because it gave her an opportunity to listen to people and help them with their problems.

So what happened to her when I left the ministry after ten years? Though she was positive and supportive during my odyssey of work and school and law practice, there was no question that leaving the ministry had created a vacuum for Judy. It was not filled until, at age forty, she entered graduate school at the University of Texas to get a master's degree in educational psychology.

Judy was excited about her new career. As her family, we were all proud of her determination to develop a career of her own. The week before her classes were to begin, she called the kids and me into the kitchen.

"You see that big white thing?" she asked. "It's called a refrigerator. For the next three years I'm going back to school. If you want something to eat during that time, look in the refrigerator. If you find something you want, you can have it. If you don't, figure out how to do without it."

We discovered that we didn't have to have home-cooked meals every day.

The day before classes began, Judy was nervous. She asked me, "Honey, would you mind riding with me over to Travis High School, where I catch the shuttle bus?"

It was almost ten miles from our house west of Austin, and I could understand her anxiety. We made our practice run, and Judy relaxed.

Monday morning, I left for the law office. Judy got in her little Volkswagen and headed for the parking lot at Travis, where she would catch an orange-and-white shuttle bus to the University of Texas. She had a ten o'clock appointment with Dr. Earl Koile, her major professor.

About nine o'clock Cornelia buzzed me and said Judy was on the line.

My wife sounded rather subdued. "Honey, could you call Earl Koile's office and tell them I won't be there?"

"Of course. Anything else you want me to tell them?"

"Just tell them I had transportation problems."

"What happened?" I inquired. "Where are you?"

"Well, a funny thing happened on the way to the University of Texas. I pulled into the parking lot and went to the corner where all these kids were standing. An orange-and-white bus pulled up, and we all got on."

"When we got to I-35, it turned south. I was a little concerned, since the University of Texas campus is north, but I figured we were going out to Ben White Boulevard to pick up some students at IRS."

"We passed Ben White Boulevard and kept going. I reached up and tapped the little girl in front of me on the shoulder. 'Could you tell me where we are going?' 'Sure,' she said. 'We're going to Southwest Texas University.' "

"You're in San Marcos?" I said, incredulous. San Marcos is forty miles south of Austin.

"Yes."

I could tell she was almost in tears. "Is there a bus back to

Austin, honey?"

"About two o'clock. I've got plenty to read."

And so began three years of graduate study. A 3.9 grade point and twenty years of practice as a psychotherapist followed.

What's the moral of that story? Don't give up if you catch the wrong bus! ■

Vive la Différence

We had been married about thirty years. Our youngest son had just left for college. And Judy uttered the words that struck fear in my heart: "I think we need to see a therapist."

I thought for a minute. Judy and our youngest, David, talked constantly, about anything and everything. I'd never minded; that meant I didn't have to say anything, which is what I did most of the time, unless a question was asked of me directly. So maybe that was the problem, I reasoned. David was gone, and there was no one to talk to but Hal. Yep . . . that had to be it.

"Who do you want to go to?" I asked, knowing she had someone in mind before she brought it up.

She told me, and I enthusiastically replied, "Okay, I'm ready. Make an appointment." We'll go two or maybe three times, I figured. Judy will talk out whatever is bugging her, and it will be over. . . .

Eighteen months later, after seeing Tom Lowry once a week, he said, "Okay, you two can make it without me."

During those eighteen months I learned more about myself and our relationship than I ever knew there was to know.

At our first session Lowry wanted us to take the Myers-Briggs Personality Inventory. That's about 300 questions that tell you if you are an introvert or extrovert or somewhere in between.

I was pretty relaxed by now. Nothing to this counseling stuff.

The second session, Tom told us how we came out on the Myers-Briggs.

"Hal, you are an INFJ. That's off-the-charts introvert."

"Introvert? I've been president of every organization I've been in since high school. Dr. Lowry, your little test must be mistaken." Actually, I thought of introverts as slightly inferior, and this verdict threatened the heck out of me.

Tom asked me what I did when I was really exhausted, when my batteries were down. Easy. I go to the woods. I get away from people. Introvert!

Now Judy, on the other hand. She's off-the-charts extrovert.

Lowry asked Judy what she wanted to do when she was exhausted. How did she "recharge"? That was easy too. She wanted to go to a party. Be around people. Extrovert!

I had the feeling that this was going to get worse before it got better.

Over the months, we opened every closet door in the house. What we found amazed me. We are so different it is incredible!

Take money. Judy's a math major. She gets her bank statement (we had separate accounts at that time), and before the day is over it balances to the penny, or the bank hears about it the next day.

Me, I put the statement aside until the next statement is due to arrive. Then I check the statement against my checkbook. If the difference is no more than $200, I change my checkbook to match the bank's record. For some reason this drives Judy up the wall.

Take being on time. When I tell someone I will be there at seven, I have given that person my word. I consider it a lack of good faith to do otherwise.

Judy doesn't think this way. Meeting some friends? They can wait. They will be there when we get there.

And then there is the way we make decisions.

Judy is like an artist. She dabs a little paint here and some there. She stands back and looks, then comes back the next day and starts the process all over. It makes no difference if this is a big decision or a small. The process is what is important.

Hal is The Judge. Line up the evidence, make a decision, and get on with it.

I'm a little embarrassed to tell you this one. Judy used to get angry with me because of my sweeping, picking up things, and putting things where they were supposed to be. "A place for everything and everything in its place" sounds almost scriptural to me. But Judy's more comfortable if there's some clutter around.

And then there's our relationship with technology. Judy has a computer in one corner of the bedroom. She sends e-mail and gets e-mail. She does the bills on the computer. You can read about my computer skills on page twenty-three of a paper written by a young graduate student from the University of Texas. She called and asked to interview me on "the use of the computer in the law office." The paragraph about me?

I met one attorney I consider to be totally computer illiterate. He had three stacks of files on his desk and he knew what he was to do that day. He said he had done it that way for 27 years and had never lost a file . . . more power to him!

Judy also uses a cell phone constantly, making appointments, checking her messages, returning phone calls. (This is done while I'm driving.) She can talk thirty minutes to a "wrong number." You couldn't pay me to have a phone in my pick-up. It's the one place no one can get hold of me.

How have we survived all these differences?

One hot Saturday morning in July I was down in the woods in front of our house cutting firewood. This is one of my favorite activities. I chew Levi Garrett and spit over the chain saw. This is about as far away from law practice as I can get. I love it!

Then I started feeling guilty. Judy was up there in the house by herself. Saturday is our day to be together, and here I was all alone . . . having fun. I turned off my chain saw and went up to the house, where I found Judy lying in a window seat reading. I confessed my guilt—the pleasure of my solitude at her expense.

She laughed and told me she had thought that morning of how peaceful it was, lying in the window seat in air-conditioned comfort. Then she thought about me working in the heat below. "I was about ready to leave and come to where you were, because I felt guilty enjoying my solitude so much!"

We embraced and laughed. Out of this experience came a gift from God . . . celebrate your differences!

By the way, we now have one bank account, and Judy handles it. What a relief! We would have done this years ago, but for my male ego that refused to admit she handled the money better than I. And Judy's allowed to "mess up" the corner of the bedroom where her computer is. As for the rest of the house, you put anything down and come back five minutes later, it's gone. In the trash.

Understanding the importance of the "process" in her decision-making, I'm no longer frustrated when she takes so long to make up her mind. Hey, I went shopping with her for a pair of shoes recently. The first place we stopped had a pair she liked. She didn't buy them until we had gone to every shoe store in the mall . . . and then returned to buy the pair she liked first.

Understanding our differences helps us to be more patient with each other. These differences have brought life, rather than irritation, to our forty-three years of marriage. This has become the statement we have repeated through the years: celebrate your differences!　■

PART TWO

Law and Some Order

When It's Okay to Hug Your Lawyer

The lady whose name had appeared on my appointment schedule stood as I entered the waiting room. She appeared to be about thirty-five, was well dressed, and from the look on her face was very distressed.

That's not an uncommon look on the faces of people who need to see a lawyer.

"I'm Hal Haralson," I said.

She offered her hand. "My name is Mary Adams."

We walked down the hall to my office, and I offered her a seat.

"You were recommended to me by another lawyer." She told me his name, but it was not one I recognized.

"What can I do for you?" I asked.

She held out a sheet of paper. It was a notice of arraignment proceedings in two weeks in Odessa. She was charged with resisting arrest.

"Why don't you tell me what happened?"

"My husband and I divorced about nine years ago," she began, "and I got custody of our son, who is now eleven. My ex-husband is a Baptist minister. He remarried and is pastor of a church near Waco. I have stayed active in my church, and that remains an important part of our lives.

"I got a job with the Austin Police Department and remained with them for seven years. I have a very good employment record. An offer came from the Federal Drug Enforcement Agency. It meant a substantial increase in salary and more opportunity for advancement, so I took the job and was assigned to the Odessa office. I liked the work and was good at it, and things went well for about three years.

"Then I began acting strangely. I couldn't sleep. I was very discouraged and everything seemed to be bad. Then that changed, and I felt invincible. I spent money on things I didn't need. I ran up excessive charge accounts—and I'm normally a very conservative person.

"My work began to suffer, and my supervisor asked me to see a psychiatrist. After extensive testing and interviews, I was diagnosed as manic-depressive. Over the next two months, I was twice committed to a private mental hospital. They were voluntary commitments. I cooperated because I was afraid I would lose my job.

"I got out and things were better. Then I began to feel very agitated and there were signs that the problem was coming back. I was really scared. One Saturday morning I was watching cartoons with my son when the doorbell rang. I opened the door and stood face-to-face with two uniformed police officers. 'We have a warrant to pick you up and take you to the State Hospital,' one of them said.

"I knew my rights and asked to see the warrant. They pushed the door open and asked me to come with them. I was afraid that if I was committed to the state hospital, I might never get out.

" 'I'm not going unless I see the warrant,' I said and began to back away from them.

"They grabbed me, put handcuffs on me, and dragged me kicking and screaming across the yard to their car.

"After spending the night in the state hospital, I was released the next day because my doctor said I did not need to be there. I was given notice of termination by the DEA. My son and I moved to Austin, where we've been living with my mother.

I've been in counseling and am working with the Texas Rehabilitation Commission for retraining.

"We've been in Austin about three months. I'd about used up my termination pay and my savings, but things were going pretty well. They told me at the Texas Rehabilitation Commission that with my college degree I stood a good chance of finding employment in another line of work."

"Where did you go to college?" I asked.

"A small West-Texas college you probably never heard of."

"Try me," I replied.

"It's called Wayland Baptist University. It's in Plainview."

"And are you feeling better now?"

"Yes. My doctor put me on lithium, and it has really made a difference. I was beginning to feel like myself again . . . and then this came." She nodded at the arraignment notice and began to cry.

"I've tried to be brave, and I've prayed and prayed. Sometimes I feel if I could have some sign from God . . . just some assurance that He knows how afraid I am and how painful this is . . . it would really help. I'm afraid they'll put me in jail at that hearing. I have no money to post bond. I have only $300, and you can have it all. Can you help me?"

"Mary, do I understand that you know nothing about me? You don't know my background?"

"No. That lawyer just said I needed to see you."

"Mary, I can answer your question about whether God knows what's happening and cares about your pain.

"What are the odds that you would see an attorney, about whom you knew nothing, and find out that he was a Baptist preacher for ten years before he went to law school? that he grew up in West Texas and graduated from the only other Baptist college in that area, Hardin-Simmons University? that he spent two years in the Army as a military policeman? that at age twenty-seven he attempted suicide and spent three months in the San Antonio State Hospital? and that he was diagnosed a manic-depressive thirty years ago and for the past twenty-one years has been on lithium?

"I think I hear God saying, 'Mary, I haven't forgotten you. I've been here all along.'"

She was overwhelmed.

"Keep your $300," I said. "I'll go to Odessa with you for the hearing."

Mary left, and I picked up the phone and called the District Attorney's office in Odessa. After a ten-minute conversation with a young lady who was the Assistant District Attorney in charge of Mary's case, she said, "I see no useful purpose in pursuing this any further. You need not come to Odessa. I'll dismiss the case."

My secretary called Mary and asked her to come in the next morning. When I told her that her case was dismissed, she could hardly speak. After she regained her composure, she stuck out her hand and asked, "How can I ever thank you?"

Ignoring her outstretched hand, I said, "It's okay to hug your lawyer." She did.

There are times when the sum total of God's dealing with us allows us to be his message to another: "I've been here all along." ■

A Mountain Man's Lesson in Ethics

I guessed the man sitting across from me to be about fifty-five years of age with no education beyond high school. His gnarled hands looked like those of a carpenter. His name was Marshall McNeil, and the knot he and his wife had tied twenty-five years before had come unraveled. He was embarrassed to tell me they were getting a divorce and looked down at his feet as he talked.

"We ain't got much," he said. "We'll sell the house and divide what's left over after we pay closing. She can have the kids, and I'll pay her child support."

I made notes as he outlined the settlement agreement.

"That's about it. Oh, one other thing. Be sure you get this in there. We owe my father $1,500. That comes out of the sale of the house before anything else. His name is Tilden McNeil."

I filed the petition the next day, and we began the sixty-day waiting period required in Texas before a divorce is granted.

Two days later my secretary buzzed me and said Mr. McNeil was on the line. I picked up the phone and identified myself.

"This is Tilden McNeil from Waverly, Tennessee. You Mr. Wholesun?" (He never did get to where he could say "Haralson.")

"Yes," I replied. "What can I do for you?"

"You represent my boy? He's getting a divorce, and they owe me $1,500. I want to hire you to get it for me."

The accent was definitely southern. But there was more. I had visions of coon dogs and mountain streams.

"I can't do that, Mr. McNeil," I said. "It would be a conflict of interest, since I already represent your son."

There was a long period of silence. I wasn't sure Tilden McNeil understood. I tried to reassure him. "I don't think you need to be concerned about getting your money. Marshall told me they were going to pay you when the house is sold."

"That don't help much." There was a note of irritation in his voice.

Two days passed. Then Cornelia buzzed me and said, "Tilden McNeil says he wants to talk to you."

I picked up the phone. "Mr. Wholesun . . . you gonna be in your office a while?"

"Yes. Where are you?"

"At the bus station. I be right out."

About ten minutes later a cab pulled up to the curb outside my office window. An old man got out. I guessed him to be nearly eighty. He was tall and slender and reminded me of the scarecrow we associate with pumpkin patches. He wore Red Hawk overalls, an old straw hat, and shoes we called "brogans" where I grew up in West Texas. As he came up the sidewalk, his steps were almost twice what I considered normal . . . as if he was walking behind a mule plowing corn.

I could hear him clear back at my office as he spoke to Cornelia. "I'm Tilden McNeil from Waverly, Tennessee. I'm here to see Mr. Wholesun."

When she buzzed, I told Cornelia to send him on back.

He stuck out his hand. "I'm Tilden McNeil from Waverly, Tennessee. You Mr. Wholesun?"

"Yes. Please have a seat, Mr. McNeil."

He looked slowly around the office. It's an 1875 country lawyer's office furnished with antiques. Above the roll-top desk is a white-tailed deer shoulder mount. There's a mounted six-pound bass among the law books.

The callused hands gripped the brim of the straw hat. Tilden McNeil was nervous. Finally he broke the silence. "Y'all do any fishin' 'round here?"

"Yes," I replied. "My boys and I fish regularly. We have several creeks and lakes that are good for bass fishing."

Tilden was quiet again. "You oughta come to Tennessee. We got bass, catfish, crappie. Some of the best fishing in the world in Tennessee."

He went on about the joys of Tennessee fishing for about ten minutes, then he changed the subject. "Y'all do any huntin' 'round here?"

"We sure do," I replied. "Texas has some of the best white-tailed deer hunting in the country."

"Y'all oughta come to Tennessee. We got bear, turkey, deer, and coon. You ain't hunted 'til you've followed coon dogs all night in the moonlight." After a lengthy discourse on the superior hunting in Tennessee, Tilden McNeil reached for the chain that hung out of his overall pocket. There was an old railroad watch on the end.

"Wa'll . . . 'bout time to get back to the bus station. Got a bus going back to Tennessee in 'bout an hour."

"Mr. McNeil, how long did it take you to get here?"

"Pert' near twenty-four hours," the old man said as he got to his feet.

"'Preciate it," he said, extended his hand, and headed for the door.

"Just a minute, Mr. McNeil. We haven't talked about your money."

"That's not what I come for. If I'm gonna do business with a man, I want to shake his hand and look him in the eye. I wanna see if he's honest. I got what I came for. I'll be goin' now."

Two years later, in a suit to give Tilden McNeil and his wife custody of their grandchildren, the judge asked me to get him some pictures of the place where the children would be living. I hired a photographer in Waverly, Tennessee to take some pictures to present as evidence.

There were two. One was of an unpainted, small house with a porch all the way across the front. It was about three feet off the ground and rested on cedar posts. There were two rocking chairs on the porch and several coon dogs lying underneath.

The other picture was of Tilden McNeil, plowing . . . those long steps outstretched. He was walking behind his mule.

By the way . . . they got the children.　■

The Will That Couldn't Be Probated

As Judy and I walked out the door of First Baptist Church in Austin, I heard someone call my name.

"Hal, I need to talk to you."

I turned to see Louise Denham, our pastor's wife. She pulled me over to the side. "Can you probate Ramsey's will?"

"Of course," I replied, and we made an appointment for the next Tuesday.

"Probate," of course, is just a fancy legal term that means to declare a will valid and genuine. It did cross my mind that this request was a little late in coming—it had been several years since the death of Ramsey Yelvington, Louise's first husband. Ramsey had been a well-known drama teacher and playwright at Southwest Texas State University in San Marcos.

I smiled as I drove home, thinking about Louise and her second marriage, to Bill Denham. I recalled the story our pastor had told us in a small group. After Bill's wife, Priscilla, died, he waited an appropriate length of time and then made a list of three women in whom he was interested. First was a high school girlfriend. He called her and found she had been married forty years and had eight grandchildren. Second on the list was the widow of Ramsey Yelvington, Louise. He never got around to calling the third one.

On Tuesday Louise sat down in my office and began talking.

"Louise," I asked. "How long has it been since Ramsey's death?"

"Seven years."

I didn't tell her, but normally we probated wills a little sooner than that.

"Did you bring the will?"

"Yes," she said and pulled it out of her purse.

The "will" was a piece of motel stationery with these typewritten words: "I leave everything I have to my wife, Louise." It was dated and signed "Ramsey Yelvington." No witnesses.

Now there is in Texas such a thing as a valid handwritten will. It's known as a "holographic will," and it must be totally in the handwriting of the testator (a fancy legal term meaning the one making the will) and may not have any typewritten statements on it. This is so you can tell if someone tries to add something after the will is written.

This piece of paper missed every qualification for a will I had ever heard of. But I told Louise I would set a hearing to admit the will to probate in San Marcos and get back to her.

The "will" lay on my desk for two weeks. (There's a fancy legal term for this also: "procrastination.") I didn't know what to do with it. Finally I set the hearing and got Louise and her daughter in the office. We went over a long list of questions I planned to ask them in order to "prove up" the will.

The day of the hearing came. We were seated at a large table when the judge came in. He was a large man, about fifty years old, wearing cowboy boots and a black robe. He looked at the file and read the will. Then he looked at me.

"Mr. Haralson, you may proceed."

I had just started my first question when the judge held up his hand.

"Just a minute, Mr. Haralson."

I had that feeling in my gut that an attorney generally gets when a judge interferes with what he is planning to do. I could not have messed up this quickly!

The judge looked at Louise. "Is this your husband's will?" he asked.

"Yes, it is," she responded.

The judge turned to me and stated emphatically, "Ramsey Yelvington is the only man who ever gave me the lead in a play. This will is approved."

As I drove back to Austin, I realized there was a lesson in this experience. Act like you know what you are doing and proceed. You never know what the other side is planning.

Or, as an old country lawyer said when asked if he had ever attempted something when it was likely he would fail, "Sure, I've put a saddle on a duck and ridden him down the street and called him a horse lots of times."

It usually works.

Try something. And act as if you expect to succeed. ■

A Rusty Lard Bucket
and One Spur

Gus McCall was eighty-eight when his wife, Gladys, died at eighty-four. They had been married over fifty years, and most of those years had been spent on their Big Bend Ranch. Gus took care of the cattle, and Gladys cooked and cleaned house.

Their kids had grown, married, and had children. There were always two or three cowboys in the bunkhouse, but mostly Gus and Gladys lived alone. Once a month they made the trek to Ft. Davis, over a hundred miles round trip. Gus was nearly blind and could no longer drive, but he knew the ranch well and got along fine.

Gus and Gladys were frugal and saved their money, and all was rather smooth until Gladys died. Then Gus sat in the lawyer's office and listened in disbelief as he was told that Gladys had made a will leaving her half of the "estate" to her grandchildren.

"What half?" he demanded. "She never done nothin' but cook."

The term "community property" was new to Gus McCall. He listened as the lawyer explained that half of everything they had belonged to Gladys, and she had chosen to leave it to their grandchildren.

Gus stumbled out onto the street. That day $300,000 worth of municipal bonds (the kind anyone can cash just by signing) disappeared from their lock box at the bank. Gus got a ride to the ranch, and no one saw him for a month.

Three years passed, and then one of Gus' sons showed up in my office and asked me to represent his children. It seems the $300,000 had not been found, and none of the land divided. As far as he could tell, it was all in the hands of a "big law firm in Odessa."

I couldn't believe that no one had deposed Gus since Gladys died, nor had anything been done to find the $300,000 in bonds. I agreed to take the case. I filed my suit and gave Gus McCall notice that I would be taking his deposition in Odessa on March 18 at two o'clock P.M.

When I got to the conference room of the "big law firm in Odessa," there were five other lawyers waiting to hear what Gus had to say.

He was nearly an hour late, and I could hardly believe what I saw when he came into the conference room. His felt hat had patches on the patches and grease and sweat all over it. It must have been fifty years old. His Levis and shirt were covered with dust and grime and did not appear to have been washed in months. Most noticeable were his run-down, worn-out boots and one spur.

After the usual introductions, I identified myself as the attorney representing his grandchildren. His look grew sullen and his half-blind eyes squinted as he tried to make out what I looked like.

"Mr. McCall, I'm going to ask you some questions, and the court reporter will take down your answers, just as if you were in court. Understand?"

"Yup."

"Mr. McCall," I continued, in a misguided effort to soften up the witness before I really got down to business, "I notice you have on only one spur."

"Yup."

"That's rather unusual. Would you mind telling me why

you are only wearing one spur?"

He looked at me as if I were a complete idiot. "You ever put your foot in the wrong boot?" Without waiting for an answer, he exclaimed, "Hurts, don't it? If you just have on one spur, you know which boot that foot goes in."

That logic was a little fast for me, so I decided to go for the heart of the matter.

"When Mrs. McCall died, there was $300,000 in municipal bonds in your lock box at the bank. Do you know anything about that?"

"Yup."

"They disappeared. Do you know about that?"

"Yup."

"Did you take them?"

"Yup."

"Are you going to tell me where they are?"

"Nope," he grunted. "When you lawyers and judges back off and leave me alone, they'll turn up."

I decided to play a long shot. "What did you do? Bury them on your ranch?"

The surprised look on his face told me I had guessed right. "Yup, but you'll never find 'em."

"Mr. McCall, you are nearly ninety years old. Has it occurred to you that you might die, and no one will know where the bonds are?"

"Yup, I thought about that. They've been hunting for that lost gold mine on my ranch for years. Someone will find 'em."

I knew what I wanted to know, so I brought the deposition to an end and dismissed Gus McCall. The other lawyers left. They knew what they wanted to know. I wondered why, for three years, no one had bothered to ask.

Two weeks later, Gus' attorney called and said he had brought the $300,000 worth of bonds into his office in a rusty lard bucket and dumped them on his desk. I suspect that lawyer told Gus after the deposition that now that he had admitted taking the bonds, he could either bring them in or the judge would carve out $300,000 worth of land from his ranch and sell it.

Either way, the grandkids would get what Gladys left them.

Lay not up for yourselves treasures on earth where moth and rust doth corrupt. . . . ■

Anything Exciting Happening in Anahuac Today?

I once had a divorce case scheduled for trial in Anahuac, Texas. Anahuac is in the swamps south of Beaumont. You can go to Anahuac, but not through Anahuac.

The other lawyer and I met in the courthouse that morning and worked out a settlement agreement in a short time. The judge asked us to prepare an order, and we went to the lawyer's office to dictate the terms to his secretary. His office was located in an old house across the street from the courthouse in surroundings that were something less than impressive. I could tell that this was not exactly a booming practice.

"Anything exciting ever happen in Anahuac?" I asked in jest.

"Well, yes," he replied. "As a matter of fact, something exciting did happen about two weeks ago." And he proceeded to tell me this story. . . .

My secretary buzzed me and said that a Mr. Abraham Schwartz was calling from New York City. I knew no one by the name of Schwartz, and I had never had a call from New York City. My curiosity was aroused.

I picked up the phone. "This is Gene Wilson, may I help you?"

me what they were doing were all the prelude to the pain of the shock. For years I wanted to bolt and run any time I lay down on a doctor's examining table.

Now I had said yes to a procedure that would duplicate much of this trip I feared so much. The doctors told me I could ask the anesthesiologist to put me to sleep gradually by the use of oral medication, so I knew I had an option. I discussed this with a few close friends and asked them to pray with me about how to deal with my fear.

When the anesthesiologist came by the night before the surgery, I decided that the way to deal with it was to face it. I prayed for freedom from the fear and chose to take the oral medication.

When the attendant came at 7:30 the next morning and strapped me to the portable stretcher, I felt a twinge of anxiety. I said goodbye to Judy and my other brother, Dale, and began the trip to the operating room. It was all the same. The lights overhead, the metal disks being strapped to my body, the voice of the doctor explaining the next step in the procedure.

"We're going to put you to sleep through the IV tube," he said. "Things should get a little foggy now." Like a TV being shut off, the sound faded and the picture went out.

When I came to in recovery several hours later, I breathed a prayer of thanksgiving. Several hours later I walked with Judy and Dale to the isolation chamber where Ken would spend about two months. He had already been given the bone marrow, and his body had accepted it.

Ken said, "I found a verse of Scripture this morning that I'd never read before. I want to read it to you."

We watched through the glass as he read over the phone so the three of us could hear. "Psalm 119:107-108: I am close to death at the hands of my enemies: oh, give me back my life again, just as you promised me. Accept my grateful thanks and teach me your desires." Ken looked at me. "Thanks."

What greater love could be expressed toward my brother than to give him the marrow of my bone?

Ken died about six months after the transplant at age thirty-five. ■

A Lesson in Humility

Trinity Baptist Church of San Antonio had always been a creative congregation. The pastor, Buckner Fanning, was constantly trying new ways of getting people to become involved in the church.

One Sunday night in 1964, Buckner announced that a group of Episcopal laymen would be leading all who were interested in "small group" worship. To be a part of this, we had to commit to be there for eight Tuesday nights.

Judy and I talked about it that night. It sounded interesting. The term "small group" was a new one to us, and we'd never seen an Episcopalian before, much less been in a worship service led by one. Pretty far out for a couple of lifelong Baptists.

So we went.

The leader was introduced: Keith Miller, an oil man from Oklahoma who had recently moved to Kerrville, Texas. The men he brought with him were new Christians, and each shared his story with the entire group. We heard from a surgeon, a dentist, the owner of a funeral home, and a jewelry maker who operated out of his garage. These men were open, honest, hilarious at times, and their stories touched us all. They were all Episcopalians.

Keith shared his own experience of searching for peace in

his life and finding it only after turning himself over to Jesus Christ. (This story eventually became Keith's first book, *The Taste of New Wine*—one of the best-selling religious books of all time.)

While we were in the circle, Keith asked if anyone wanted the group to pray for him or her. Judy raised her hand. "All right," said Keith. "Let's all pray for Judy."

She was really embarrassed. She didn't know Keith had meant here and now.

Then we divided into groups of eight, where Keith had us go around and answer a set of questions. The questions were nonthreatening and simple in the beginning. It took several weeks to get through them, and as we gave our answers and listened to others a bond of trust began to form among us.

We were impressed with the small-group process, and eventually we formed one of our own: a Baptist couple, an Episcopal priest and his wife, and a Methodist couple. Wow. We Baptists were really being influenced by those Episcopalians.

Keith was named director of Laity Lodge, the Butt Foundation Camp near Leakey. He invited Judy and me to participate in a weekend and asked me to speak. It was one of the first times I spoke publicly about leaving the ministry, my suicide attempt, and dealing with manic-depression. We developed a close friendship with Keith and participated in a number of teams in churches that asked him to lead conferences. This usually consisted of my speaking and Judy having a smaller part in the programs.

After the publication of his first book, Keith left Laity Lodge to spend more time speaking and writing. Bill Cody was named director at Laity Lodge, and he asked us to go with him to lead a Faith at Work conference at St. David's Episcopal Church in Austin.

We were honored to be on the program, as St. David's is a large church and there would be a lot of people there. I began working on my remarks before we got to Austin.

The team met with Bill prior to each session and talked about what had happened in the last one and who was to speak next. We were building toward the final session, which would be the largest number of people. Bill had not called on me yet, so I figured that meant he was saving me for the last and most important gathering. At the team meeting Bill looked at my wife and said, "Judy, I would like you to speak at the final session."

That was it! I wasn't going to be called on for anything.

Judy made notes on the back of a couple of napkins. When Bill introduced her, she stood and read "Woman's World," by Judy Haralson.

> My world is made up of Mondays, Tuesdays,
> Wednesdays,
> Thursdays, Fridays, Saturdays, Sundays, Mondays
> Washing, ironing, cooking, cleaning, churching
> Mending clothes, turning down radios, wiping noses and
> bottoms
> Answering telephone and doorbells
> Letting dogs in and letting dogs out
> Taking children to and bringing children from
> Fixing food, making beds, mopping floors
> Rejoicing, crying, listening
> Rejoicing with Jill when her cat has kittens
> Crying with Brad when his kite string breaks
> Listening to David's tales of Sesame Street.
> I must communicate with my husband
> Share with my neighbors
> Empathize with my friends
> Organize myself, my home, my children, my husband,
> the women at church
> On and on, endlessly, my world goes
> Then Jesus steps into the uttermost parts of my world
> and speaks
> He speaks through little mouths, teary eyes, hurt looks
> He speaks through closed doors, trusting hands,
> unuttered wishes
> He speaks through David as we make a cake
> "Me help, Mommy, me help"

"David, if you wouldn't help so much I could get it done
    a lot better, in half the time"
Then I listen as the great God says to me
"Judy, if you just wouldn't help so much I could get it
    done better, in half the time."

She sat down to a stunned silence. It was the high point of
the weekend.

My ego was bruised. No one got to hear me speak. I had
been upstaged by my wife.

My ego was repaired as time passed. My pride in my wife
and my respect for her abilities has continued to grow through
the years. So has my respect for Episcopalians. ■

A Sears and Roebuck Christmas

The fortieth reunion of the 1953 graduating class of Loraine High School was held in the senior citizens center—the only place in town large enough to hold us. After all, we were the largest graduation class in the history of Loraine High School . . . all twenty-three of us.

Actually we were the first baby boom, born in 1935 after the Depression was over and folks decided it was okay to start having babies again. Thirteen members of the class had begun in the first grade and gone through twelve years of school together. As we went around the circle at our reunion, sharing our "most memorable experiences" with the other class members, I knew what I would tell.

On my left sat a tall, elegant woman with long gray hair: Beth Narrell. I fell in love with Beth Narrell in the fall of '42, way back in the second grade. As Christmas approached, I searched for a way to make my feelings known. Finally I decided on a pin, which I ordered from the Sears Roebuck catalog. It was heart-shaped with an arrow through the heart—"fourteen-carat gold-filled" with three "ruby-like" stones. I raced to the mailbox every day waiting for the package to arrive, and it finally did. The most beautiful piece of jewelry ever made. It cost me $3.73. I was certain that giving this symbol of my love to Beth would solidify our relationship forever, but it didn't. She married Bobby Price, the football hero, and we went our separate ways.

As I shared this story at the reunion, Beth picked up her purse, reached inside, and took out my Sears Roebuck pin. As she pinned it on her lapel, there wasn't a dry eye in the house.

Go ahead . . . do something tangible to show your feelings for someone you love. The cost is not important. ■

A Price Tag on Love?

It began with a visit to Young Life's Trail West Lodge in Colorado. Charlie Little, an architect from Dallas, and I "cut class" one morning and hiked up the canyon. The scenery was magnificent. The water rushed over the rocks in the bottom of the canyon, and the slopes were dotted with abandoned mines.

"What a place to bring our boys," I remarked.

"Let's do it," Charlie replied.

We made our plans and put the date on our calendar. When I got home and told Brad, my ten-year old son, he was so excited he could hardly contain himself. Two full days of hiking and fishing. He read brochures, looked up Colorado in the atlas and encyclopedia, and became more excited with each passing day.

Tension mounted as our departure date neared. Then came the ill-fated telephone call from Charlie . . . the press of business . . . he couldn't make it. We set the date back three weeks. Brad was brave, but his letdown was evident. I really hurt with him in his disappointment, and realized my excitement was almost as great as his.

As the new date approached, we prepared the gear. Brad had a thousand questions. Will we see any deer? How cold is it? Will it snow? My love for my son and his spirit of adventure was overwhelming as I anticipated the trip with him. The week came, and I touched base with Charlie by phone. All systems were go.

It was Wednesday—tomorrow was the big day. I was trying, without much success, to read a legal document, when my buzzer sounded: "Charlie Little is on the line."

I picked up the phone. "Little, if you are calling to tell me you can't go, you may as well take out a large insurance policy and buy a burial plot. You're gonna need both."

"I'm sorry, Hal. It's a big contract, and I just can't leave."

There were the usual apologies and pleasantries, and it was over. I hung up the phone, feeling as though someone had kicked me in the gut. The thought of telling Brad was even worse. I just didn't think I could do it. The original plan had been that Brad and I would drive to Dallas, pick up Charlie and his son, and drive all the way to Buena Vista. On impulse I reached behind my desk and picked up the phone. There was a Thursday afternoon flight from Austin to Colorado Springs. We could return on Monday.

The cost was nearly $400. We would have to rent a car in Colorado Springs and drive to Buena Vista, probably another $100. My law practice was only two years old at the time, and we didn't have that kind of money. But with the kind of plunge that is characteristic of my decision-making process, I made the airline reservations. Where would we stay? We could take no camping gear on the plane. I decided we would just cross that bridge when we got there. Judy concurred with my decision and took us to the airport.

How do you describe the wide-eyed excitement of a ten-year old boy on a 737 with his dad, flying to Colorado on a trip that is especially for him? Words aren't adequate. How fast are we going? How high are we? Will we get to eat? What if something happens to the engine? Yeah, I know it won't, but what if it did?

The questions kept coming. We landed and rented a car for the two-hour drive to Buena Vista. Brad's excitement increased as we crossed the Arkansas River and pulled into the Young Life property in the foothills of the Rocky Mountains.

Then he was disappointed. There was no snow.

The lady at the desk at Trail West told us that a Nazarene college was having a faculty retreat there that weekend, but there were extra rooms. We could stay there and eat our meals with them. It was an affirmation I needed, and I gave a silent prayer of thanks.

We took our fishing gear and started after trout as soon as we finished breakfast. Brad and I have fished for bass together since he was four years old, but our ignorance about trout fishing was monumental. I had a feeling the man in the sporting goods store in Buena Vista sensed this. His list of what we "needed" sounded like he was outfitting a pack trip to climb Mt. Everest.

We hiked and fished all day. First the Arkansas River. No trout. Then Beaver Dams high in the Rockies . . . one trout . . . length three inches . . . or maybe two.

Getting tired of "fishing," Brad said, "Let's see what's at the end of the road."

"Great idea, let's go," I replied, and we piled into the car. After what that car went through the next six hours, I imagine the Hertz people are still looking for us. We went higher and higher. Brad's breath sucked in with excitement as we rounded a corner and saw an abandoned mining town. Visions of run-away mine trains and crusty old miners danced through our heads as we explored the old buildings. I was having as much fun as Brad. The road got narrower and narrower as we went higher, till finally we were above the timberline. The road ended when it became an abandoned railroad track.

As we looked out across the Arkansas River Valley from 10,000 feet, Brad said, "Dad, it must have been this way when God created it." I began feeling okay about the trip.

We barely made it back for supper. The day had been long and exciting. After supper and a phone call to Judy, we hit the sack. Saturday morning we woke up to find that God had apparently ordered up the only thing that was missing for my son. Snow! It looked like another world!

We hiked up the canyon above Trail West. Brad saw several deer, and we explored the abandoned mines. I stretched my poncho across a portion of a log cabin at noon, and we ate our lunch and watched the snow fall. The beauty of God's creation defied description.

That afternoon we made our way back to the lodge and headed for Colorado Springs, where we checked into the Holiday Inn. We went to the restaurant, and Brad registered surprise when I answered yes to his question, "Dad, can I have a steak?"

"Boy, how about that! Me and Dad, climbing mountains, flying in jet airplanes, and eating steak. I'm the luckiest guy in the world."

That night we propped ourselves up in bed and watched television. Then, lights out. I thought Brad had gone to sleep. That's when my mental adding machine began. Plane tickets $409. Car $110. Trail West $90. My stomach knotted.

Then, out of the darkness: "Dad, are you awake?"

"Yes."

"Dad, you're the greatest father on earth. I love you. Good night."

Silence. He was asleep.

I learned something from this trip about time alone with my children. About doing something very special with only one of them. About being extravagant. Brad's "I love you" reminded me of the great love God expressed as He reached down to share His Son Jesus with each of us. Sometimes extravagance says "I love you" more clearly than any other expression. It builds memories. It says: "You're important to me." It says: "I love you."

What does it cost to build a memory? I knew that night that this one hadn't cost too much. ∎

Index

A Personal Note From the Author

More than to just entertain, Cook Communications Ministries hopes to <u>inspire</u> you to fulfill the great commandment: to love God with all your heart, soul, mind, and strength; and your neighbor as yourself. Towards that end, the author wishes to share these personal thoughts.

I once had just spoken to a group of people, when a lady came up to me and said, "You know what you are? You are a story teller." I like that. I try to present my message through telling stories. A lawyer tried to trick Jesus (they'll do that) by asking, "Who is my neighbor?" In so many words, Jesus said, "Let Me tell you a story." The Parable of the Good Samaritan would become one of the most famous stories ever told. The stories for *Gentle Mercies* cover many subjects, but I think they all touch on heart, soul, mind, and strength when it comes to living the Christian life in this fallen world.

Heart

One story that is particularly close to my own heart is that of the broken hearts of the parents in "Being There." To me this story serves as a back-drop to illustrate the coming of God in Jesus Christ. Also, many of my stories are about the heart of a seeker making his or her way into the arms of an ever-patient God, as illustrated both in *A Grease Rack Prayer* and *Lassoin' a Cattleman*.

Soul

Many of my stories connect well with soul of the struggling psalmist, who clung to the promise of God's gentle mercies:
Withhold not thou thy tender mercies from me, O Lord: let thy lovingkindness and thy truth continually preserve me.

Psalm 40:2

Mind

There is much in this collection of stories about the mind and what it is to struggle against life's circumstances and even against God. For instance, there's the mind of a minister so depressed he plans his own death in "Sunday Morning Suicide." And of course, there's my own battle with depression—one that is not likely to end until the Lord takes me home. I think these stories can cause one to take a closer look at what it means to have the mind of Christ, especially when we come to understand that ours are fallen.

Strength

And then there are so many stories about strength—strength that comes from knowing Christ. Sometimes we have the privilege of lending strength to others, as was the case in "It's Okay To Hug Your Lawyer." But I think maybe her story can lend us strength too as we see a young mother who searches for a way to provide for her son, even after she had lost her job. In fact, I think the characters of most all of these stories lend strength to others—I know that's the case for me.

Dear Lord, among these 50-or-so stories, I pray that each reader may find one that brings confidence and awakens his or her personal faith in You.

Ten Years a Minister, Six years a Business Man, 30 years a Lawyer...
These are Stories of Faith in Faded Blue Jeans

GENTLE MERCIES
By Hal Haralson

Hal Haralson has delivered a powerful collection of stories from his life, ministry, and over 30 years of law practice in *Gentle Mercies*. Ordinary life lived in extraordinary manner is the essence of this first compelling book by Haralson. He openly chronicles God's work in the many trials and challenges he has faced through years as a pastor, businessman, and practicing attorney. Readers will benefit from his honesty and wisdom in areas such as dealing with a "call" to and from ministry, dealing with mental illness, family, expressing love, dealing with bad habits, forgiveness, friendships, humor, and much more.

Jimmy R. Allen, Former President of the Southern Baptist Convention has this to say about *Gentle Mercies*. "Along the way we are introduced to cowboys struggling toward belief, bag ladies leaving fortunes for mental patients, bankers hearing voices, and pickup trucks taking on personalities of their own. [This] is a must read for folks eager to stay in touch with the reality of authentic faith in an increasingly virtual reality world." Foy Valentine, founding editor of *Christian Ethics Today*, says "Here is stardust in boots and jeans. From the overflow of a richly eventful lifetime, Haralson's writing is profoundly human - wise, warm, tender, earthy, insightful, honest, gloriously authentic, and deeply spiritual."

Haralson reveals God's goodness, mercy, and grace as a master story-teller in the transforming narratives.

ENDORSEMENTS

"Like Jesus' parables, Haralson's stories are subterfuge, slipping in under your guard and seizing you with such truth, grace, and extravagant love, you will never be the same!"

George Cladis,
Presbyterian Minister,
Darien, Conn.

"How is it that Hal makes me laugh and cry at the same time? Maybe it's the cowboy in all of us that loves campfire stories."

Father Keith Hosey,
Catholic Priest & Director,
John XXIII Center

About the Author

Hal Haralson is a frequent contributor to *Christian Ethics Today* and has been a practicing attorney for more than 30 years. After time of army service and 10 years as a Baptist preacher, Hal struggled through serious depression and was eventually diagnosed as manic-depressive. In the many years since, Hal has championed to break down the stigma attached to mental illness. The National Mental Health Association awarded Hal the Clifford Bears Award and he has also received the Dole Foundation Award for his work with the mentally ill. Hal graduated from Hardin-Simmons University with a bachelor's degree in history and minor in Bible in 1957. Hal also holds a law degree from the University of Texas (1971) Hal has practiced law as a solo practitioner in Austin, Texas for over 30 years.

To learn more about Hal and his book contact him at
www.gentlemercies.com
or write him at
P.O. Box 90909, Austin, TX 78709-0909
or haralsonj@prodigy.net